9 Requirements for Quality Research and Academic Papers

I0410294

By

Sa'idu Sulaiman

Email: saisulaiman@yahoo.com

Published in 2016

By

CreateSpace, USA.

ISBN-13: 978-1539329756

ISBN 10: 1539329755

TABLE OF CONTENTS

Preface i

Chapter One

Introduction 1

Chapter Two

Academic Writing, Creativity and Types of Academic Papers 5

Chapter Three

Understanding the Research Process and the Research Proposal Guidelines 10

Chapter Four

Selecting and Stating Research Problems 15

Chapter Five

Reviewing the Literature 20

Chapter Six

Stating the Objectives, Scope, Significance and Limitations 35
of a Study

Chapter Seven

Formulating Research Questions and Hypotheses 39

Chapter Eight

Choosing a Research Methodology 45

Chapter Nine

Defining Terms and Compiling References 71

References 75

PREFACE

Intellectualism and scholarship will cease to flourish without research and academic writing in form of books, thesis, journal articles, conference papers, etc. In the same vein, the unborn generation will not benefit from the intellectual achievements of the present generation without academic writing. Half of the research work to be undertaken by a researcher is considered done by the time a researcher becomes familiar with the essential requirements for quality research. Similarly, writing quality research papers for seminars, conferences or for publication in academic journals is accomplished with success when the writer meets the requirements for producing such papers. These requirements are also crucial when it comes to writing a research proposal that is acceptable to research project supervisors in academic institutions and to donor organizations and agencies providing research grant.

The author has extracted or modified portions of his earlier book *Researchers' Companion,* 2nd edition, he also added certain features to this book which make it straightforward, these include beginning each chapter with specified objectives to guide readers and enable them focus their attention towards achieving the objectives.

This book guides potential researchers through nine essential requirements for writing quality research proposals and academic papers with less stress and frustration. As some academic papers are research based, the book does not treat 9 requirements for quality research separately from the requirements for quality academic papers.

The book begins with an introduction which covers the meaning, types and importance of research. This is followed by features of academic writing and its relationship with originality and creativity, and then a typology of academic papers/journal articles. In the remaining chapters, the book delves into the explanation of the 9 steps required for writing quality research proposals with some useful advice and precautions, where needed, and down—to—earth examples related to education, social and management sciences, and in certain cases, the natural sciences. The book is also a guide to writing research based journal articles and conference papers.

The 9 requirement are

1) Explaining some forms of contribution to knowledge and 5 types of academic papers;
2) understanding the research process;
3) following research proposal guidelines and format;
4) selecting and stating a research problem;
5) reviewing the literature;
6) Stating the objectives, scope, significance and limitations of a study;
7) formulating research questions or hypotheses;
8) adopting a research design/methodology;
9) **defining terms and compiling references.**

Chapter One

INTRODUCTION

Chapter Objectives

By the time you finish reading this chapter, it is expected that you will be able to:

- Define the term *research*.
- Explain the difference between research methods and research methodology.
- State and explain three types of research.
- Explain 4 points on the importance of research.

1.1 Definition of Research

The term research refers to purposeful and planned activities aimed at discovering facts about a given phenomenon. The phenomenon could be unemployment among youth, failure in examinations, high intensity of rural-urban drift, misconception of the ideal goals of life, etc. Facts to be investigated about a phenomenon could be its features, essence, problems, relationship with other phenomenon, etc. For Selltiz, Wrightsman and Cook (1976:2) to do a research means to "search again, to take another more careful look to find out more". So a research is more than a cursory look at a phenomenon because it is a process involving a set of ordered activities meant to facilitate a more reliable discovery of facts.

It therefore goes without saying that one needs to acquire knowledge about research methods before being able to carry out these activities. There is a distinction between research methods and research methodology. Method refers to a way of doing something, for instance, there are methods of teaching and methods of international settlements used in international trade. Research method is a way of carrying out all the research activities that form the research process. A methodology on the other hand refers to a set of methods used in working at something, for instance, one needs to adopt a methodology for identifying distressed banks, or for classifying agricultural produce into grades A, B and C, by using a given criteria. A research methodology is therefore a philosophy adopted by a researcher with which he/she undertakes the activities that constitute the research process. Assumptions made by a researcher and the criteria used in interpreting data and reaching conclusions are all part of research methodology.

1.2 Types of Research

There are different ways of categorizing researches. Researches could be divided into two major categories: pure and applied. A pure research, which is also called basic research, involves developing and testing theories and hypotheses that are intellectually interesting to the investigator and might thus have some social application in the future (Bailey 1994: 24). Most of researches undertaken by students and lecturers, and also reported in academic journals belong to the pure research category.

An applied research deals with large scale studies covering a wide area of interest such as education, drug addiction, population census and human development indicators. Researches usually carried out by governmental and non-governmental organizations and by research consultants fall under applied research. Applied researches require more funding, time and research personnel because of their wide coverage. A census of private schools in Egypt with a view to finding their number, student population, teachers' qualifications, etc, is a large scale study requiring a lot of money and the findings will have practical significance to policy making in the education sector. This research is an example of an applied research.

Research is also categorized in terms of the following:

1. Exploratory studies: These studies are made to explore the nature of a given phenomenon at an initial stage so that subsequent and more careful studies could be guided by the outcomes of the exploration. A baseline study on the number and ages of children in a given community meant to guide establishment of schools or marketing of toys and children wears is an example of exploratory studies. Exploratory studies are made to satisfy a desire for a better understanding of a phenomenon. They are also used to test the feasibility of using a suitable methodology for a further and more detailed and careful study.

2. *Explanatory studies:* These are concerned with finding explanations to *why* questions, for instance, why the electorates voted for Peter instead of Paul during election or why entrepreneurship is more prevalent in a given community than in other communities ?

3. *Descriptive studies*: These are carried out to describe situations, events and institutions. Examples of these studies are the description of product consumption rates in certain towns, the description of age, income and occupation profiles of members of a given community, description of the behavior patterns of people living with HIV /AIDS, etc.

1.3 Importance of Conducting Research

For people that take things for granted without making any effort to understand why they exist and how they could be improved or replaced with better alternatives, research work is a waste of time and resources. The following points underscore the importance of research:

a). Without researches people will continue to regard the familiar as inevitable and the unfamiliar as inconceivable. Cynics will remain contented with old ways of doing things and will not bother about the need for discovering new ways and new ideas that will make life easier. Such people do not even imagine an alternative conception of the world in which they live.

b). Another purpose of conducting researches is to scrutinize accepted beliefs and discover a better alternative. The religious beliefs of most people, for instance, are simply based on what they acquire and imitate from their parents, not on investigations about the genuineness of existing faiths or a comparative analysis of their tenets.

c). Frontiers of knowledge cannot be expanded without research, for instance, the knowledge about the deadly disease called AIDS caused by the HIV virus has been expanding since the discovery about its existence. This becomes possible because of the attention which researchers pay to the disease and the availability of research grants.

d). Research facilitates rapid economic growth and development of communities and nations through discovery and invention of more efficient methods of production, distribution and exchange of goods and services, or of addressing problems.

Chapter Two

ACADEMIC WRITING, CONTRIBUTION TO KNOWLEDGE AND TYPES ACADEMIC PAPERS

Chapter Objectives

By the time you finish reading this chapter, which covers the 1st requirement for producing quality research and academic papers, it is expected that you will be able to:

- List and explain 3 features of academic writing.
- Explain the relationship between academic writing, originality and creativity.
- State some key features of creative people.
- State some forms of contribution to knowledge.
- Explain five (5) types of academic papers.

Features of Academic Writing

Gocsik (2004) explains three features of academic writing: first, academic writing is writing done by scholars for other scholars. Being a scholar requires that you read, think, argue, and write in certain ways. Second, it is devoted to topics and questions that are of interest to the academic community. When you write an academic paper, it should be of interest to other people in the academic community; it must be more than a personal response. Third, academic writing should present the reader with an informed argument. If an academic piece fails to inform, or if it fails to argue, then it will fail to meet the expectations of the academic reader.

Through there are other means of communicating ideas, knowledge, and traditions, such as oral tradition, music, paintings, news papers, magazines, tales and quasi-academic texts, they are not as reliable as academic writing. Academic writing involves critical examination, analysis and evaluation of facts on the basis of evidences as to their sources; validity of methods of used to access and verify them, and the competence and integrity of authors.

Academic writing is necessary to every student, lecturer or scholar. It is the means for effective teaching and learning, students need it in order to write essays, dissertation reports and papers. Lecturers use it to groom students and assess their academic performance and to meet the partial requirements for promotion or appointment to academic positions. Scholars use academic writings to publish their thoughts, discoveries, views and other contributions to knowledge, or to refute, correct or modify what other scholars have published.

Academic Writing, Originality and Creativity

Academic writing requires originality, that is, the quality of being new or different from what already exists, and also of not being imitated or copied. A contribution to knowledge is novel and original when it is unprecedented in the available literature; it is an independent replication of an investigation in a different setting or when it is a modification to an already existing contribution. Originality requires creativity, which differs from intelligence. Syed (nd) states that of all the abilities of human beings, the creative faculty has always been considered as the most mysterious; in many cultures, creativity is believed to come from a divine or at least an unconscious source; and that highly creative people have the following characteristics:

a) They tend to be introverted.
b) They need long periods of solitude.
c) They seem to have little time for what they regard as the trivia of everyday life and social activity.
d) They tend to be strongly intuitive and more interested in the abstract meaning of the outside world than in the way it appears to the senses.

e) Creative people may have poor human relationship and may avoid social gatherings.

f) Creative individuals appear to be relatively free from conventional restraints and are not particularly concerned with what other people think of them.

Forms of Contribution to Knowledge

Members of academic staff in institutions of higher learning are required to conduct researches and publish them in academic journals. This is done to ensure their contribution to knowledge and to keep them abreast with developments in their fields. A contribution to knowledge needs to be original. There are various forms of contribution to knowledge which include the following (Sulaiman, 2013):

(a) Critique, review, commentary, exegesis and synthesis of existing knowledge.
(b) Discovery of a new knowledge or phenomenon.
(c) Explanation of a new phenomenon.
(d) Finding new solutions to a problem.
(e) Creation of a new procedure, principles, system or model for doing something or addressing an issue.
(f) Analysis of an existing phenomenon (comparative, descriptive, prescriptive, historical, philosophical, trend and cost-benefit analyses, etc) to provide new or additional knowledge about it.
(g) Translation work meant to increase people's access to existing knowledge.

Types of Academic Papers

Based on the descriptions of types of journal articles made in four write-ups, namely, Types of Articles Published, Types of Articles in Scholarly Journals, Types of journal manuscripts and Guidelines on Writing a Philosophy Paper, (see their respective sources in the references), there are at least five different types of academic papers accepted for publication in journals. They are as follows:

1. Empirical /Research based Paper

This type of paper has in-depth review of the literature and development of hypotheses and includes full introduction, methods, results, and discussion sections.

2. Case Study Research Article

A case study research article reports specific instances of interesting phenomena. It could include an in-depth study of a single case or several cases, description of the methodology used for gathering data, a description of the statistical analysis of the data, and a discussion of the findings, including suggestions. The goal of *Case Studies* is to make other researchers aware of the possibility that a specific phenomenon might occur.

3. Conceptual/Theoretical Article

This is an article containing or referring to a set of new or established abstract principles related to a specific field of knowledge. It does not normally contain original research or present experimental data. A conceptual/ theoretical article should be strongly grounded in the relevant theoretical literature in functional areas such as education, organization behaviour, psychology, etc. It is important that conceptual/theoretical research articles focus on cutting-edge topics and present new insights.

4. Review Article

This is an article summarizing the results of studies or experiments, often attempting to identify trends or draw broader conclusions. It provides a comprehensive summary of research on a certain topic, and a perspective on the state of the field and where it is heading.

5. Philosophy paper

A philosophy paper consists of the reasoned defence of some claim made by the author, not a mere report of your opinions or those of the philosophers studied or discussed. A philosophy paper usually begins by putting some thesis or argument on the table for consideration. It then defends the argument or thesis against existing criticism, offers reasons to believe the thesis, contrasts the strengths and weaknesses of two opposing views about the thesis and discusses what consequences the thesis would have, if it were true, among others.

Chapter Three

UNDERSTANDING THE RESEARCH PROCESS AND THE RESEARCH PROPOSAL GUIDELINES

Chapter Objectives

By the time you finish reading this chapter, which covers the 2nd and 3rd requirements for producing quality research and academic papers, it is expected that you will be able to:

- List and explain activities that constitute the research process.
- Explain the concepts *hypothesis* and *research question.*
- State the category of research design that is more suitable for the natural sciences; and the one that is more suitable for education, arts and the social sciences.
- Explain the concepts *data reduction* and *data coding.*
- Mention the types of statistics used for descriptive studies.
- Mention the types of statistics used for testing hypothesis and making inferences.
- List the typical components of a research proposal guideline.

3.1 Understanding the Research Process

Research undertaking is not a single activity but a process involving many activities leading to a final result. For a quantitative research, the research process involves the following activities:

(a) Selecting a research problem

Selecting a research problem and describing it in clear language are the most important tasks in conducting a research. This is because the objective, scope and means of achieving the objective must all reflect the research problem. If a problem is not properly 3defined,

---

the remaining activities that form the research process may be unrelated to the problem which the research is meant to address.

b) Literature Review

The literature refers to the works of other people, published and unpolished, which are related to a research topic or a research problem. In research work, the task of literature review involves reading the works related to one's topic with a view to giving them a critical look and determining their relationship with the topic under study.

c) Formulation of research questions or hypotheses

A hypothesis is a proposition that is stated in a testable form. It predicts a particular relationship between research variables. Bailey (1994:42) defines a hypothesis as "a tentative explanation for which the evidence necessary for testing it is at least potentially available". Hypotheses provide direction to research and prevent the review of irrelevant literature and data collection; they also provide the framework for stating conclusions at the end of a study.

Research questions are questions to which a study seeks to provide answers. They guide research work, prevent collection of irrelevant data and serve as terms of reference for research work. Studies that do not require the formulation of hypotheses can be undertaken with the help of research questions.

c) Adopting a research design/methodology

A researcher, like a professional tailor, needs to adopt a particular design that will give his work the desired shape or form. A tailor adopts particular design for a particular dress by bearing in mind the nature of the dress, the materials needed and the income and needs of the ultimate user. A researcher too needs to consider the nature of his research topic, the availability of resources, time needed for the research and the ultimate goals or purpose for conducting it.

There are two main categories of research designs. There are designs for a *quantitative research*, which is more suitable for the natural sciences; there are also a set of designs for the *qualitative research*, which are more suitable for education, arts and the social sciences.

There are several methods of collecting data with reasons for adopting them in a study, which need to be known by a researcher before writing a proposal. There are also several methods of analyzing data with different types of statistics which a potential researcher needs to be conversant with especially in terms of knowing the appropriate statistics for each research design.

(d) Data collection

A researcher collects data with a view to testing hypothesis or answering research questions. The data could be primary or secondary. It is primary when it is used for the purpose for which it is collected. Data used for a purpose other than for which it has been collected is called a secondary data.

(e) Coding and analyzing data

Both primary and secondary data collected by a researcher need to be summarized and presented in a suitable form to permit analysis and inference. The responses contained by hundreds of questionnaires, for example, have to be summarized and sometimes coded or reduced. Data reduction is the process of reducing data to some form for suitable analysis. Coding can take the form of assigning numbers to expected responses (pre-coding) or to obtained responses (post-coding) and is necessary especially when a computer is to be used to analyze the data.

Data analysis takes many forms which depend on the use for which the analysis is made. If the analysis is required for descriptive purposes or for answering research questions, descriptive statistics could be used to analyze the data. Percentages, frequency distribution, mean, median, mode standard deviation and variance could be used for descriptive purposes.

However, if the purpose of the analysis is to test hypothesis and make inferences, statistics of inference need to be used, so the appropriate statistical techniques could be z -test, t-test, chi-squared (x^2), correlation coefficients, contingency tables, and the rests.

(f)   Interpretation of results and drawing conclusions.

The interpretation of statistical results and the drawing of conclusions are also part of data analysis. The results obtained from a study need to be discussed by means of comparing or contrasting them with the findings of similar studies, describing their policy implications and showing need for further studies, where applicable.

3.2 Research Proposal Guidelines and Format

Research proposal guidelines are written guidelines made available to people seeking research grants or students in universities, colleges and polytechnics. They specify what is required or recommended before a research proposal is accepted. Typical components of a research proposal guideline include the following:

- Executive summary
- background to the study
- problem statement
- justification for the study
- research objectives
- significance the study
- scope of the study
- limitation of the study
- literature review
- methodology
- expected results
- implementation plan
- budget
- references
- etc

Executive summary, justification for the study, implementation plan and budget are applicable to research proposals submitted to organizations providing research grants or contracts.

The format of the research proposal refers to design, arrangement and layout of the contents of the proposal. It is important to note that research proposal guidelines and formats differ from one academic institution to another and also from one organization providing research grants to another. One, therefore, needs to obtain the research proposal guidelines and formats relevant to the desired research activity, and also to follow them strictly. Doing this, is one of the essential steps of writing an acceptable research proposal.

Chapter Four

SELECTING AND STATING RESEARCH PROBLEMS

Chapter Objectives

By the time you finish reading this chapter, which covers the 4th requirement for producing quality research and academic papers, it is expected that you will be able to:

- Identify factors influencing one's selection of a research problem and subsequently a research topic.
- Write out a number of research problems in relation to chosen areas of research interest.
- Coin research topics from specified research problems.
- Take precautions in relation to selecting problems or topics that are not researchable.

4.1 Selecting a Research Problem

Research is conducted to address problems of knowledge gaps that limit the understanding of a given phenomenon such as a rise in unemployment, decline in morality, and also determining relationship between maturity and examination marks obtained by pupils, factors leading to failures of an organization, a system or a policy, etc.

Many factors influence one's selection of a research problem and subsequently a research topic. These include:

1. Researcher's interests, hobbies and curiosity.
2. Researcher's values, aspirations and the school of thought to which he/she is inclined.
3. Exposure to academic works, institutions, system, people and events. A student who is well exposed to these things can easily choose a research problem related to any of these.

4. Time factor: some research problems like the relationship between age and verbal communication may require a longitudinal study (studying a particular individual for some years). Others may require a cross sectional study (studying and comparing different individuals in a single period).
5. Research methodology adopted for data collection, analysis and test of hypothesis could also influence the choice of a research problem.
6. Unit of analysis chosen: some studies involve few respondents while others involve a large sample of respondents. A researcher has to consider the unit of analysis he/she intends to use before selecting a research problem.

4.2 Stating a Research Problem

The experiences gathered by the author of this book in the capacities of a project supervisor, external moderator and a member of project defense panels, indicate that a significant number of students find it difficult to state a research problem. One common mistake made by students is to list all the problems faced by an organization or a system they are studying and regard them as the research problem. A student writing a project on *Marketing of Banking Services in a Deregulated Economy: a Case Study of Pan African Commercial Bank*, for instance, will mention all the problems which affect the operations of the bank under the heading "Problem Statement". This is not what is meant by problem statement. Problem statement simply means the need for the study. This could be a number of statements or questions on how the bank markets its services under the conditions of a deregulated economy, which prior to undertaking the research, the researcher could not answer appropriately. This constitutes a problem or some knowledge gap, which banishes when the research is carried out.

A good research problem needs to ask questions concerning the relationship between the sets of variables to be correlated, compared or observed. In addition, dependent variables need to be distinguished from independent variables while the scope of the problem needs to be set within feasible limits.

Let's have examples of two hypothetical research topics and their respective problem statements.

First topic: *Relationship between Age and Conservatism among Farmers in Saromet Community*

Problem statement: This study will investigate the relationship between the ages of adult farmers in Saromet community and conservatism, which is defined as resistance to the new methods of storage of farm produce introduced to the community by the AgriNet organisation in 2013.

Second topic: *Baseline Study of Entrepreneurial Undertakings among the Fulani People of Kambola*

Problem statement: This study will determine the types of entrepreneurial undertakings of the Fulani people of Kambola, the sources of capital for the undertakings as well as the educational background and training needs of the entrepreneurs.

Other examples of problem statement include determining:

i. Determining the relationship between students' interest and performance in Geography lessons;
ii. Investigating the effect of drug addiction on crime rate among youth;
iii Finding whether there is a correlation between share prices and share holders' educational background;
iv. Assessing the impact of waste water on soil fertility; and
v. Finding the prevailing conditions of primary school buildings in a given community.

4.3 Coining a Research Topic

The moment a researcher is able to select a research problem the coinage of the topic becomes very easy. The topic has to be framed in such a way that it portrays the research problem, and in addition, it has to be narrowed down to indicate the scope of the study. Let's have an illustration using the following research problem: *determining the effect of drug addiction on crime rate among youth.* The topic could be formulated and narrowed down in stages as follows:

Stage 1: The Effect of Drug Addiction on Crime Rate among Youth in Germany
Stage 2: The Effect of Drug Addiction on Crime Rate among Youth in Berlin City
State 3: The Effect of Drug Addiction on Crime Rate among Youth Working in Berlin Restaurants.

At the first stage, the topic is too broad; at the second, it has been limited to the capital city of Germany but it still requires a further narrowing. At the final stage, the topic is narrowed further to what can be handled conveniently because the respondents are to come from restaurants in the city. However, a large scale study can be made on the wider topics, but this will require more time and funds.

4.3 Some Advice and Precautions to Secure Success in Selecting a Research Topic

In selecting a research topic, one should consider the following:

1. The topic should be original: Do not write on what others have written. However, a replication of research is allowed, for instance, if a student wrote on the topic given above (stage 3) another can write on the same topic provided that youth from other settings are used in the study (e.g. youth attending high schools in Miami, USA, or receiving military training in Nairobi, Kenya).

2. The topic should be of interest to the researcher.

3. The topic should be feasible: One should consider the possibility of having access to required data, availability of time and resources, etc.

4. One needs to also understand that not all topics can be subjected to research. One cannot, for instance, undertake a longitudinal study on the relationship between age and dexterity of dwarfs from the period of infancy (0-2 years) to the age of senility when they become confused and unable to look after themselves (at about 90 years of age and above) due to the length of the period of study. One cannot also use a research to determine who is a saint among the residents of a community, because their present moral behaviour can change at any time while some people can appear to be morally excellent but are inwardly wicked. But a study on the number, age, income level and occupations of people that exhibit the behaviours or characteristics of saints, as given in sacred religious books, is possible.

5. Lastly, the likely problems to be encountered in conducting a research and the extent to which they can be surmounted also need to be considered.

Chapter Five

REVIEWING THE LITERATURE

Chapter Objectives

By the time you finish reading this chapter, which covers the 5th requirement for producing quality research and academic papers, it is expected that you will be able to:

- Explain the term literature review.
- Explain the benefits of literature review in research.
- List the qualities of a good literature review.
- Explain the term *plagiarism*.

5.1 The Task and Benefits of Literature Review

In the context of research work, the term *literature* refers to the works of other people, published and unpublished, which are related to a research topic or research problem under study. These works include research reports published as articles in academic journals and as textbooks, and also unpublished thesis submitted to academic institutions or research reports submitted to organizations providing research grants. Others are web and blog based articles from reputable authors, print and electronic dictionaries and encyclopedia, newspapers and magazines, documentaries, etc.

In research, the task of literature review involves reading works related to one's topic with a view to giving them a critical look and determining their relationship with the topic under study. A researcher is expected to critically review the literature related to his/her research topic. To review the works of other people means to re-evaluate them or have another look at them. The review should go beyond copying or summarising what other people have written. One should criticise or asses definitions, introduction, organisation of report, depth of analysis, clarity of expressions, etc, made by other writers. As for the review of related studies conducted by other people, one should re-evaluate them in relation to the problem statement, research questions or hypotheses formulated, scope of the studies, methodologies and sampling techniques adopted, the findings, generalizations made, conclusions reached, recommendations given, etc.

Literature review facilitates the understanding of a phenomenon under study, familiarity with related works done by other researchers, the methodologies they used, and identification of existing knowledge gaps which future studies will fill, etc. After the conduct of a study, the reviewed literature is also useful in discussing results as it allows for comparison of results of previous studies with those of the current study. For literature to provide these good benefits, it needs to be

- Relevant to the topic under study.
- Well understood and digested.
- Reliable.
- Current.
- Wide in scope and coverage.
- Sourced from a variety of sources (books, journals, magazines, websites, etc) and authors.

5.2 Advice and Precautions

It is advisable to review current literature and necessary to acknowledge all authors whose works have been cited by simply stating their surnames and years of publication wherever their ideas, views, findings, definitions, etc, appear in the literature review. Direct words used by authors should not be reproduced unless when they are being quoted. In this case, the words quoted must be put between opening and closing inverted commas. Long quotations (of three lines and above) need be to be presented in the form of indented paragraphs.

There is the need for a researcher to refrain from plagiarism when reviewing the literature or making a citation in any apart of the research report. Plagiarism is defined as "the copying of ideas, text, data and other creative work (e.g. tables, figures and graphs) and presenting it as original research without proper citation"(http://www.informs.org/Find-Research-Publications/Journals/Author-Portal/Publications-Policies/Guidelines-for-Copyright-Plagiarism). Plagiarism has also been defined as

> an act or instance of using or closely imitating the language and thoughts of another author without authorization and the representation of that author's work as one's own, as by not crediting the original author" (http://dictionary.reference.com/browse/plagiarism)

5.3 A sample of a Literature Review

The following is a sample of a literature review for a proposed study entitled *Socio-Cultural Factors Affecting Entrepreneurial Intentions among College of Education Students in Northern Nigeria*, which the author of this book has written in 2015. It is reproduced here only for illustration purpose.

Introduction

The literature review begins with the description of the state of unemployment and other problems hindering the development of entrepreneurship in Nigeria. It then covers reasons why people choose to be self-employed and the conceptual and theoretical framework, which includes the impact of socio-cultural factors on entrepreneurial activity as well as some entrepreneurial intention models. A number of entrepreneurial intention studies have also been reviewed.

Unemployment and other Problems Hindering the Development of Entrepreneurship in Nigeria

The National Bureau of Statistics (2011) reports an increasing trend of lack of interest by the emerging younger generation of Nigerians in highly labour-intensive work such as agriculture and factory work in preference to white collar jobs. The national unemployment rate increased to 23.9% in 2011 compared to 21.1% in 2010 and 19.7% in 2009. The Bureau's definition of unemployment covers persons aged 15 – 64, who during the reference period, were currently available for work and also seeking for work but were jobless. Being employed means being engaged in the production of goods and services, thereby contributing to the gross domestic product in a legitimate manner. In 2006, there were 7,067,051 unemployed persons but in just five years the figure had jumped to 16,074,205 (National Bureau of Statistics, 2011).

Onu (2013) also notes that there is an unprecedented increase in the number of unemployed graduates from tertiary institutions in Nigeria which requires diversifying the economy and encouraging practical acquisition of skills through inculcating the spirit of self–reliance in students. Entrepreneurship education is about developing understanding and capacity for the pursuit of entrepreneurial behaviours, skills and attributes in widely different contexts. It is, therefore, necessary to expose all students to entrepreneurship education which can be effectively stimulated in schools.

Despite strong economic growth, youth's full-time unemployment rate for 2006 –2008 in Nigeria was put at 55.9%. While countries like Japan, China, India and Korea, have joined the community of industrialized nations by strengthening their small scale industries, Nigeria is yet to understand the relevance of this sub-sector (Ojeifo, 2013).

Unachukwu as reported by Sulaiman (2014) identifies some problems hindering the development of entrepreneurship in Nigeria. These include the lack of substantial funds for providing entrepreneurial education, financing start ups and expansion of business; unaffordable equipment and technology and pressure from some parents who prefer their children making money within a short period of time. There are also the absence of well developed curriculum that emphasizes initiatives to increase accountability; and poor entrepreneurial attitude due to complacence among the Nigerian populace. Other problems hindering the development of entrepreneurship in the country are lack of data for entrepreneurship education; inadequacy of facilities like good roads, electricity, access to information, water supply, etc; lack of culture that respects risk taking as a necessary condition for creating value from knowledge; and the absence of fully developed linkages between research centres and universities with the outside world.

Even though there has been substantial research on psychological and economic approaches to entrepreneurship, the influence of social and cultural factors on enterprise development remains understudied (Thornton, Ribeiro-Soriano and Urbano, 2011).

Reasons why People choose to be Self-employed

There are many reasons why an individual chooses to be self–employed. Ogundipe, Kosile,Olaleye and Ogundipe (2012) enumerated the following as some of the reasons why people choose to be self–employed:

a) Desire to have economic freedom: Some people choose to be self–employed on the basis of economic opportunity to receive compensation based on merit.

b) Desire to have autonomy: The desire to be free from being subservient to others, to be independent, to be one's own boss could be the reason for developing entrepreneurial intention.

c) Desire to exert authority, to have power and to make decision may have gingered some people to embark on entrepreneurship exploits.

d) Self–actualization: The desire to be self–actualized, to realize one's dreams, to create something, to take advantage of one's creative needs could also be the reason for having an entrepreneurial intention.

Conceptual and Theoretical Framework

Entrepreneurship involves commitment of resources, under conditions of uncertainty and risk, to transform some novel ideas into products or services that have value (Siraj, 2013). Entrepreneurship has also been described as the process of producing something new with value through creating sufficient time and effort with social risk, and resulting to reward and personal satisfaction (Daluba and Odiba, 2013). Adeboye and Olubela as reported by Abefe-Balogun and Nwankpa (2012), define entrepreneurship as the process of creating something new with value by devoting time and effort and assuming financial, psychic and social risks, and receiving monetary rewards, personal satisfaction and independence. This definition includes the reasons for being an entrepreneur. Finally, Unachukwu, (2009) states that entrepreneurship is more than being smart, it is the ability of a person to collaborate with others and act in the face of new opportunities, and to possess innovativeness, key skills and talents.

On the nature of entrepreneurship, Gilder (2012) argues that entrepreneurship is the launching of surprises, and that free human enterprise is unpredictable as it resists every econometric model and socialist scheme. It makes no sense to most professors, who attain their positions through systematic acquisition of credentials. He further explains that wealth does not consist of only a stock of materials but chiefly includes creativity, attitudes, moral codes and mental disciplines, which are endowments that can neither be confiscated from the people having them nor redistributed to benefit the people lacking them. Creativity is the foundation of wealth and all progress comes from the creative minority.

Onuoha (2013) states that entrepreneurs are agents of economic and technological development, in other words, they are wealth creators, while Invancevict *et al*, as reported by Onuoha (2013) see the entrepreneur as a person that assumes the risk of creating incremental wealth by making the commitment of providing value to a product or service.

Entrepreneurial intention has been defined as one's willingness to undertake entrepreneurial activity, or to become self - employed. In social psychology, intention is regarded as the most immediate and important precursor of behaviour, and therefore, a strong predictor of entrepreneurial activity (Ogundipe *et al*, 2012).

From the above statements, it is clear that entrepreneurship is about value creation requiring innovativeness, key skills and talents, and done under conditions of uncertainty and risk. Secondly, the nature of entrepreneurship indicates that skill acquisition and provision of capital are not the only requirements for successful entrepreneurship. Creativity, attitudes, moral codes and mental disciplines, which are endowments that can neither be confiscated from the people having them, are very essential. Lastly, entrepreneurial intention, which is simply one's willingness to undertake entrepreneurial activity, or to become self employed, is a strong predictor of entrepreneurial activity.

Impact of Socio-Cultural Factors on Entrepreneurial Activity

Until recently, culture has not received much attention in entrepreneurship research. Entrepreneurship research on culture can be divided into three types: firstly, studies meant to find out how culture produces entrepreneurship; secondly, studies on how entrepreneurship produces culture, and lastly, studies aiming to develop new (culture) theory in order to expand the theoretical horizon (Brøgger, 2013). With regards to empirical research, studies on the relations between culture and entrepreneurship are relatively new (Thurik and Dejardin, 2011).

As reported by Thornton, Ribeiro-Sarino and Urbano (2011) much of the research in entrepreneurship that considers cultural variables followed Hofstede's work. This work shows how culture is manifested in various forms and how national culture affects cultural values at individual or societal levels. According to this view, the quantifiable dimensions of cultural differences across societies are uncertainty avoidance, individualism, masculinity and power distance. Uncertainty avoidance stands for certainty and discomfort with unstructured or ambiguous situations, while individualism stands for a preference for acting in the interest of one's self and immediate family, instead of acting in the interest of the society in exchange for its loyalty and support. Power distance is the recognition or acceptance of inequality in position and authority among people. Masculinity represents a belief in materialism and decisiveness rather than service and intuition. Researchers have, on the basis of Hofstede's concept of culture, generally hypothesized that entrepreneurship is encouraged by cultures that are high in individualism and masculinity, and low in uncertainty avoidance and power–distance.

Writing on three theories that provide an analytical framework to investigate the relationship between culture and entrepreneurship, Thurik and Dejardin (2011) submit that entrepreneurship is measured in terms of firm creations or business ownership and self–employment rates, and that it varies over time. While some variations are linked to the level of technological development and new markets, variations across countries and regions seem to be the result of institutional and cultural contexts. They further explain the three theories as follows:

> a) *The aggregate psychological traits approach:* there is a link between individual values and beliefs, on the one hand, and individual behaviour on the other. According to this approach, for a given country, the more individuals with entrepreneurial values there are in a society, the more individuals will display entrepreneurial behaviour.

> b) *The social legitimation or moral approval approach:* here the focus is on the impact of social norms and institutions on the conduct of the society at large. According to this view, a higher entrepreneurial activity is found in societies where the entrepreneur is seen to have a high social status. The education system recognizes and supports entrepreneurship while tax incentives encourage business start–ups.

> c) *The dissatisfaction approach:* this approach is basically different when compared to the first two approaches. Differences in entrepreneurial activity across nations and regions are linked to differences in values and beliefs between potential entrepreneurs and populations as a whole. So in a predominantly non—entrepreneurial culture, a clash of values between groups may drive potential self–employed persons into actual self–employment.

Entrepreneurial Intention Models

Entrepreneurial intention has been defined as one's willingness to undertake entrepreneurial activity, or to become self –employed (Ogundipe *et al*, 2012). Attitude is often explained in entrepreneurship research through reported desire to be self–employed or own a business (Kapasi and Galloway, 2014). Understanding factors related to entrepreneurial intention is very important because intentions are reliable predicators of entrepreneurial action (Ogundipe *et al*, 2012).

Izquierdo and Buelens (2008) state that previous studies have contributed to the entrepreneurship literature by using intentional models to explain the entrepreneurship phenomenon. These include the Shapero's entrepreneurial event (SEE) model where entrepreneurial intentions depend on three elements: a) the perception of the desirability; b) the propensity to act; and c) the perception of feasibility, and the Ajzen model in which intentions are explained by: a) subject's attitudes toward the behaviour; b) subjective norms; and c) the subject's perception of behavioural control. There is also Bird's model which considers entrepreneurial intentions to be based on a combination of both personal and contextual factors. There is also a further development of the Bird's model by Boyd and Vozikis which added the concept of self—efficacy taken from the social learning theory. Finally, there is the Davidsson's model which suggested that entrepreneurial intentions can be influenced by the following factors: a conviction, defined by general attitudes (change, competence, money, achievement, and autonomy) and domain attitude (payoff, societal contribution and know how). Conviction, in turn, is related to personal variables including age, gender, education, vicarious experience and radical change experience (Izquierdo and Buelens, 2008)

As Ogundipe, *et al*, (2012) report, the Ajzen model seems to be popular in intention studies. It is called the Theory of Planned Behaviour. Based on the premise that much human behaviour is planned, the theory assumes intention as the immediate antecedent of behaviour. As a result, the model stresses that three key attitudes predict intention: attitude towards an act, the subjective norm, and lastly, the perception of the behavioural control. The first attitude is towards the act. This attitude is based on the perception of the person of what he/she might think of as a desirable outcome. If someone expects that the outcome of the act is getting him or her in a better position, it will be more likely that he/she will perform the act. The second attitude is that of the subjective norm. The subjective norm reflects the extra personal influence on the decision–maker.

Scholten *et al.* in Ogundipe *et al* (2012) explain three key attitudes that predict intentions towards entrepreneurship as follows:

Personal attitude means the degree to which the individual holds a positive or negative personal valuation about being an entrepreneur. It includes not only affective (I like it, it is attractive), but also evaluative considerations (it has advantages).

Subjective norm measures the perceived social pressure to carry out—or not to carry out entrepreneurial behaviours. It is the perception that "reference people" would approve of the decision to become an entrepreneur, or not. So the image of entrepreneurship is the subjective norm reflecting one's beliefs about the expectations of others and the motivation to comply with these expectations.

Perceived Behaviourial Control is defined as the perception of the ease or difficulty of becoming an entrepreneur. It could include not only the feeling of being able, but also the perception about controllability of the behaviour. Therefore, the more favourable the attitude and subjective norm and the greater the perceived control, the stronger the intention of an individual to become an entrepreneur.

Basu and Virick (2008) have also explained the three elements in the Theory of Planned Behaviour, namely, attitudes, subjective norms, and perceived behavioural control. They define attitudes as beliefs and perceptions regarding the personal desirability of performing the behavior, which are in turn related to expectations regarding the personal impact of outcomes resulting from that behaviour. Subjective norms or perceived social norms are one's perceptions about the values, beliefs, and norms held by people whom one respects or regards as important and one's desire to comply with those norms. They describe perceived behavioural control as the personal belief about being able to execute planned behaviour and the perception that the behaviour is within the decision maker's control.

Kapasi and Galloway (2014) have tested the validity of the Theory of Planned Behaviour in the context of the actual experiences of actors as they perceive the influences and circumstances of their entrepreneurship (or lack of it). Their study proved that the Theory of Planned Behaviour has much to contribute in explaining entrepreneurship and the role of agency within the decision to become an entrepreneur.

Entrepreneurial Intention Studies

Helmy, Abbass, and Kortam (2014) have investigated the entrepreneurial intentions of Egyptian students by means of a comparative study between profitable and social contexts. Results of the study have proved the validity of the model they have developed as well as the effectiveness of Shappero and Sokol's model (perceived feasibility and perceived desirability) in predicting and explaining the commercial and social entrepreneurial intention.

Being part of culture, religion can influence one's decision to become or not to become an entrepreneur. With the interest of finding an answer to the question, "Is Religion Associated with Entrepreneurial Activity?" Henley (2014) used correlation and regression analysis to test hypotheses concerning the nexus as well as potential mediating effects of societal and state regulation of religion and levels of economic prosperity and growth. Results of the study indicated that there is a significant association between the evangelical-pentecostal-charismatic movement (EPCM) form of Christianity and rates of entrepreneurship across nations. Secondly, entrepreneurial activity appears to be negatively associated with higher levels of government regulation of religion.

Ogundipe *et al,* (2012) investigated the impact of entrepreneurship education courses and career guidance which students were exposed to on their entrepreneurial intention. They used a sample of two hundred and six (206) graduating students from Departments of Guidance and Counselling and Business Education of Lagos State University, Sandwich programme. The findings show that the knowledge and skills derived from the two courses have impact on entrepreneurship intention of the respondents, but the Counselling students show stronger entrepreneurship intention than their Business counterpart. Thus career guidance facilitates development of intention to become an entrepreneur.

The goal of the study conducted by Mungai and Ogot (2012) was to determine whether entrepreneurial activities vary among gender across the ethnic cultures, and whether the cross cultural ethnic differences are apparent between genders within the separate cultures among Kenya's ethnic groups. They carried out a survey of 120 participants using a stratified sampling technique to ensure inclusion of equal male and female participants in all the four ethnic groups, namely, Luo, Kikuyu, Kalenjin and Kamba. The 5-point likert scale was used. The outcome of the study is that there were neither significant gender differences on community perception of entrepreneurship nor the extent on the presence (or absence) of personality traits associated with entrepreneurship. Secondly, it appears that for the communities studied, ethnic cultural influences play a greater role in women's propensities towards entrepreneurship.

Basu and Virick (2008) studied the relationship between ethnicity and entrepreneurial attitudes, subjective norms, and perceived behavioural control. The ethnic composition of the sample indicated that 45.5% of the respondents were Asian, 23.6% were Caucasian, and 14.6% were Hispanic/Latino. The results indicated no differences in subjective norms and perceived behavioural control among students from different ethnicities. However, for attitudes, it was found that Caucasians have the most positive attitudes to entrepreneurship (mean =.48), followed by Asians (mean = .30) and Hispanics/Latinos (mean=-.09).

A group research conducted by Ahmed, Nawaz, Ahmad, Shaukat, Usman, Wasim-ul-Rehman, and Ahmed (2010) was aimed at determining the impact of personal traits, demographic characteristics and entrepreneurship education on entrepreneurial intentions of university students of Pakistan. Data was collected from a sample of 276 students from five major universities. Results show strong relationship between innovativeness and entrepreneurial intentions, but some demographical characteristics, that is, gender and age, were insignificant with the intentions to become entrepreneurs. However, prior experience, family exposure to business and level of exposure inclined students to become entrepreneurs.

Another group research conducted by Nasurdin, Ahmad and Lin (2009) tested a causal model of affective factors (role model, social identification and social norm), perceived desirability, and entrepreneurial intention in the context of Malaysia. Data for the survey was derived from a sample of 237 Malaysian working adults, students, and unemployed people. The results show that role model and social norm were positively and significantly related to entrepreneurial intentions but the direct effect of social identification on entrepreneurial intentions was not significant. The mediating effect of perceived desirability was found to be partially supported. Findings from the study demonstrate the significance of role models and social norms as means of promoting entrepreneurial ventures and addressing the problem of increasing unemployment among Malaysians.

Conclusion

From the literature review, it is clear that entrepreneurship is about value creation requiring innovativeness, key skills and talents and done under conditions of uncertainty and risk. Secondly, there is a growing interest among researchers in investigating the impact of culture on entrepreneurial intention. Thirdly, the theory of planned behaviour is still acceptable to many researchers despite being formulated by I. Ajzen since 1991. Lastly, there has never been a study on the impact of socio-cultural factors on entrepreneurial intention of college of education students at national or regional level in Nigeria.

....

From the sample literature review, one could see how a researcher could have deep understanding of entrepreneurial intention and the models used to investigate it. The methods used in previous studies on entrepreneurial intention also become manifest in the literature review, so are their findings which could be useful in discussing the result of the proposed study. All the cited works in the above literature review have been included in the complied references, which do not need to appear in this book.

Chapter Six

STATING THE OBJECTIVES, SCOPE, SIGNIFICANCE AND LIMITATIONS OF A STUDY

Chapter Objectives

By the time you finish reading this chapter, which covers the 6th requirement for producing quality research and academic papers, it is expected that you will be able to:

- State the objectives of a study, which reflect its title and problem statement.
- Explain the scope and significance of a study.
- Mention and explain four dimensions of the scope of coverage for a study.
- Identify the limitations of a study.

6.1 Objectives of the Study

The objectives of conducting a study need to be derived from the problem statement. One may include "to provide recommendations based on the findings of the study" as the last objective. For a supposed topic: *Relationship between Rewards and Job Performance among Textile Workers in Oldham, Manchester,* the objectives could be as follows:

a) To determine the types of rewards used by textile firms in Oldham from 2004-2014 to improve the performance of their workers.
b) To determine the frequency of using rewards by the textile firms to improve the performance of their workers.
c) To determine the relationship between monetary reward and job performance of textile workers in the study area.

d) To determine the relationship between non-monetary reward and job performance of textile workers in the study area.

e) To provide recommendations based on the findings of the study.

6.2 Significance of the Study

This is the importance of the study or the benefits it will provide after the completion and production (and sometimes publication) of the report. A researcher is expected to explain the significance of the study in terms of filling knowledge gaps in the field of study, and in calling attention of relevant authorities and policy makers directly linked with the subject matter or issue covered by the study.

6.3 Delimitation of the Study (Scope of Coverage)

Under this section, a researcher is required to "build a fence" around his/her topic by explaining the length, breadth and depth of the subject matter or issues dealt with in the study. The period to be covered by the study can also form part of the scope of coverage. One of the advantages of doing this is that the researcher will have a definite focus which could be maintained throughout the research process, from problem statement to conclusion and recommendations. Another advantage is that the researcher could defend the inclusion or non-inclusion of certain aspects of the topic in the research. The following is an example of a statement of the scope of the supposed research topic:

> The study is concerned with the types of monetary and non-monetary rewards, and the frequency with which they are used by textile firms in Oldham from 2004-2014 to improve workers' performances. It is also concerned with the determination of relationship between the rewards offered and job performance of textile workers in study area.

This statement of scoped of coverage indicates that the researcher is making definite statements on the subject matter of the study, the population from where the research subjects will come, the location and the time frame within which the study is to be conducted. The table below shows these dimensions.

Table 6.1 Dimensions of Scope of Coverage

Dimensions	Relevant sections of the statement of scope of coverage
Subject matter	The study will focus on the types and frequency of usage of monetary and non-monetary rewards, and the determination of their relationships with job performance.
Population from where the research subjects will come	It will involve textile workers only.
Location	The workers must have worked with the textile firms located in Oldham.
Time	The workers must have worked within the period 2004 — 2014.

9 Requirements for Quality Research & Academic Papers

6.4 Limitation of the Study

This is the shortcoming associated with the adoption of particular research methodologies and techniques as well as reasons for not choosing other methodologies and techniques. For any research one is conducting, the design, sampling technique, data collection method, statistical tools of analysis, etc, could have certain shortcomings which one could not overcome due to time factor, financial constraints, the nature of the research subjects, etc. With illiterate research subjects, for instance, one has to rely on interviews which limit the use of a large sample sizes in gathering data. Stating the limitations of your study does not mean you are giving up yourself to your assessors and critics; it is rather an indication that you have a mastery of the research process.

Chapter Seven

FORMULATING RESEARCH QUESTIONS AND HYPOTHESES

Chapter Objectives

By the time you finish reading this chapter, which covers the 7th requirement for producing quality research and academic papers, it is expected that you will be able to:

- List and explain different types research variables.
- List and explain different types of relationships existing between research variables.
- Explain the concepts *hypothesis* and *research question.*
- Formulate hypotheses from a given research topic or problem.
- Formulate research questions from a given research topic or problem.

It is pertinent to begin this chapter by explaining different types of research variables and the different types of relationships existing between them before going into the formulation of research hypotheses and research questions. This is because research variables are the building blocks of research hypotheses and research questions while the relations between them determine the nature or focus of a research problem.

7.1 Types of Research Variables

Some studies are conducted with a view to establishing a relationship and or causality between variables. Studies on the impact of home background on learning ability, the effect of tax policy on capital budgeting decision or the relationship between age and conservatism are all oriented towards establishing and understanding relationships between variables.

Variables simply refer to determining factors or change agents. Age, sex, home background, tax laws, conservatism, corporate goals, intelligence and aggression are examples of variables. No research involving variables can be meaningful, reliable and acceptable unless the researcher is able to differentiate a dependent variable from an independent variable, and to identify the type of relationship between them.

Types of Variables

1. *Independent variable:* This is a variable which is essentially responsible for or determines another variable. In certain cases, especially in natural sciences, the independent variable causes a change in another variable. A slimming tablet, for instance, is an independent variable which reduces body size.

2. *Dependent variable*: This is the variable which is susceptible to influence from an external determining factor (i.e. the independent variable). If, for instance, a study reveals that young people frequently read sports magazines, the reading of the magazines is the dependent variable. Being young makes one to read sport magazines but reading the magazines does not make one young.

3. *Intervening variable:* When two variables A and B are correlated such that A does not directly cause B but it causes C, and C cause B, C is called an intervening variable. A change in the minimum qualification for contesting in elections from Senior School Certificate to National Diploma could indirectly increase demand for advanced level textbooks by directly increasing students' admission into higher institutions to obtain diplomas. In this example, the increase in students' admission is the intervening variable through which the change in the minimum qualification indirectly increases demand for the textbooks. A relationship between two variables occurring due to an intervening variable is called *spurious relationship*. Thus, there is a spurious relationship between the change in the minimum qualification for contest and the demand for advance level textbooks.

4. *Extraneous variable:* This is a variable that distorts the true relationship between the variables in which a researcher is interested. Let's assume a researcher is investigating the relationship between teachers' income and their demand for laptop computers at a time when a businessman is supplying the market with fairly-used iPad tablet computers at attractive prices. This supply of substitute products is an extraneous variable that will distort the relationship being studied by the researcher.

7.2 Types of Relationship between Variables

Rosenberg (1984) provides detailed explanation of the types of relationships between research variables and distinguishes between the following types of relationships.

1. *Symmetrical relationship:* This exists when two variables do not influence each other. Body weight, for instance, has no influence on brand selection for safety matches; just as using a particular brand of safety matches does not affect the body weight of the user.

2. *Reciprocal relationship:* This exists when two variables influence each other. A good example is the relationship between a person's kindness to his neighbour and the neighbour's kindness to him, or the relationship between social class and organizational membership.

3. *Asymmetrical relationship:* This relationship exists when one variable influences another variable (the dependent variable). Most research efforts are geared towards variables having this kind of relationship. The relationship between age and conservatism is an example of an asymmetrical relationship.

When dealing with research variables, a researcher is more often than not, interested in understanding what causes what or what determines what, etc. Two things need to be stated here. First, causation as Bunge observes,

...is not a sufficient condition for understanding reality... scientific explanation is, in short, explanation by laws – not necessarily explanation by causes (quoted by Rosenberg, 1984:72).

Bunge adds that determination involves a necessary connection between two variables, and causation is just one of such connection. He also argues that the strict doctrine of causality disregards the fact that all known actions are followed by reactions, that is, the effect always reacts back on the input (the independent variable) unless the latter ceases to exist (cited by Rosenberg,1984).

Secondly, to understand the direction of determination, two factors need to be considered. There is the time order of the variables, so what happens later cannot be responsible for what comes earlier. The second one is the fixity or alterability of variables. Fixed variables, like age, race and sex are uninfluenceable, so they cannot be regarded as dependent variables (Rosonberg, 1984).

7.3 Formulation of Hypothesis and Research Questions

With a clear understanding of the variables to be studied and the kind relationship they have, formulation of research hypotheses or questions and the choice of the appropriate means of testing the hypotheses or answering the research questions, become easy. While research questions are needed to guide the conduct of both quantitative and qualitative studies, hypotheses are suitable only for the former.

A researcher can use research questions only, hypotheses only or a combination of the two depending on the research designs adopted and the nature of the topic. It is always appropriate to use hypotheses, which are assumptions on the effect of a measurable variable over another variable, in an experimental research design. Research questions and hypotheses need to be related with the problem statement and the objectives of the study, in fact, they could be derived from the latter.

Hypothesis

A hypothesis is a proposition that is stated in a testable form. It predicts a particular relationship between research variables. Bailey (1994:42) defines a hypothesis as "a tentative explanation for which the evidence necessary for testing it is at least potentially available." Hypotheses provide direction to research and prevent the review of irrelevant literature and data collection; they also provide the framework for stating conclusions at the end of a study.

A null hypothesis, usually denoted by H_o assumes no relationship between variables. An assumption made against the null hypothesis denoted by H_a or H_1 is called an alternative hypothesis. When the collected data supports the null hypothesis it is accepted, and when the data disagrees with it, it is rejected. Below is an example of the null and alternative hypotheses for a study investigating the effect of the use activity method in teaching Social Studies by using the quasi-experimental research design:

H_o: activity method of teaching has no effect on learning outcome
H_1: activity method of teaching has effect on learning outcome

Concepts used in formulating a hypothesis have to be well defined and measurable, for instance, learning outcome has be stated in measurable terms such as test scores, grades, etc.

Proving or disproving a hypothesis is not a guarantee that the research finding is absolutely correct. Scientific findings have limitations because, as Babbie (1986:402) rightly observes, "Nothing is ever proved scientifically". Selltiz, Wrightsman and Cook (1976) also state that neither hypothesis nor theories can be verified in the ultimate sense.   Harris (1979) also explains the limitations of empirical findings, for instance, an investigator's pre-conception and motives influence his/her choice of methodology of investigation and this affects the outcome; there are also filtration mechanisms like social pressure, prejudice and psychological delusions that operate between our sensation of the world and our perception of it. Thus knowledge acquired through the use of the senses is not as reliable as knowledge sourced from God's revelation, which is flawless and perfect.

Research Questions

Research Questions are questions to which a study seeks to provide answers. They guide research work, prevent collection of irrelevant data and serve as terms of reference for research work. Studies that do not require the formulation of hypotheses can be undertaken with the help of research questions. The questions are answered after collecting relevant data, and conclusions are drawn based on the answers. A study appraising the services of a rural branch of a commercial bank in the last five years could have the following as research questions:

1. Which services were provided by the branch in the last five years?
2. How was the branch offering each category of service?
3. Who were the main beneficiaries of the services?
4. Which problems militated against the effective provision of the services?
5. How could the identified problems be minimized?

Finding answers to above questions with the use of research data will shed light on the work of the branch and contribute to knowledge on rural banking.

Questions aimed at determining relationships between variables can also be formulated, for example:

1. Are scores in the Senior School Certificate Examination related to scores in a semester examination in a polytechnic?
2. Does high pay enhance employee performance?
3. Do training expenses incurred by a firm reduce wastage of its raw materials?

Chapter Eight

CHOOSING A RESEARCH METHODOLOGY

Chapter Objectives

By the time you finish reading this chapter, which covers the 8th requirement for producing quality research and academic papers, it is expected that you will be able to:

- Define the term *research design.*
- Explain the concepts *quantitative research* and *qualitative research.*
- Explain the difference between quantitative research and qualitative research.
- List and explain the limitations of both quantitative and qualitative researches.
- State and explain the different types of quantitative research designs.
- State and explain the different types of qualitative research designs.
- State and explain the different probability sampling techniques.
- State and explain the different non-probability sampling techniques.
- List and explain types of data and data measurement scales.
- Mention and explain the methods of data collection.
- State and explain the methods of data analysis.
- Chose an appropriate research design, sampling method, data collection and analysis methods for your planned study.

8.1 Definition of a Research Design

A research design has been defined by Selltiz, Wrightsman and Cook (1976:90) as the arrangement of conditions for the collection and analysis of data in a manner that aims to combine relevance to the research purpose with economy in procedure.

As we shall see in this chapter, quantitative and qualitative researches differ considerably in terms of approaches and the worldviews supporting them. Despite this, Bryman (1988) in Hughes (2006) argues for the use of both so that one can get the 'best of both worlds'. A researcher should ignore the politics of legitimacy and evidence surrounding the contending worldviews by using any of the approaches or combining them, depending on the research goal and other relevant factors.

8.2 Quantitative Research Designs

Quantitative research designs were originally developed to study natural phenomenon. Later, they were extended to the social sciences. A quantitative research is an empirical research with data existing in the form of numbers. It is concerned with collection and analysis of data in numeric form with emphasis on the use of large-scale and representative sets of data often presented as 'facts' (Hughes, 2006). Quantitative research paradigm is based on the positivist worldview, which sees reality or truth existing outside the researcher, the research situation and the subjects involved (Sambo, 2005). Positivism in research is a belief that the researcher and the researched are independent of each other. Citing the work of Burns (2000), Hughes (2006), states the important elements of quantitative research. They include control of variables to identify causes of a phenomenon, operational definitions of concepts to clear confusion and ambiguity, replication to ensure reliability of research outcomes, and hypothesis testing. Quantitative research designs include the following:

1. *The Experimental design:* In an experimental research design a researcher is able to compare a control group of subjects (a group not receiving treatment) and an experimental group which is exposed to a treatment. This is done so that a cause and effect relationship can be established. An investigation of

the effect of a brand of fertilizer on crop yield, for instance, requires the use of an experimental design, with crops in one farm treated with the fertilizer and crops in another farm (the control group) not given this treatment. All other factors and conditions affecting crop yield will be the same so that the yields from the two farms can be compared. There are different forms of experimental designs classified under quasi-experimental (pre-experimental) and true-experimental designs. Designs in the former category are called pre-experimental because they fail to control most of the causes of internal invalidity of experiments while the latter control most of these causes. Both categories have been explained in detail by Sambo (2005).

2. *Formal methods:* Formal methods such as econometrics also form part of the quantitative research. Econometrics is the application of mathematical and statistical method to economic data to provide empirical content to economic theory. Regression analysis has for long been the main tool of econometrics.

3. *Numerical analysis:* This is applied to the fields of engineering and the physical sciences. At a later stage, especially with advancement of computer applications, numerical analysis was extended to other academic disciplines. The main goals of the analysis are the design and analysis of techniques to give almost accurate solutions to hard problems such as weather prediction, more precise calculation of values of stocks by investment companies, use of sophisticated optimization algorithms by airlines to decide ticket prices, fuel need, tasks to be performed by crew members, etc, (http://en.m.wikipedia.org/wiki/ Numerical _Analysis).

Hughes (2006) states the following limitations of the quantitative research:

a) Not all variables can be controlled especially when dealing with human experiences.

b) Human beings do not respond to experiment in the same way as lifeless matter in the physical sciences.

c) Mechanistic approach of the quantitative research tends to exclude notions of freedom, choice and moral responsibility.

d) Quantification can become an end itself; the unique ability of people to interpret their experiences, construct their own meanings and act on them are not taken into account.

e) Quantitative research assumes that the so—called facts determined from studies are true and same for all people all the time.

f) The restriction of controlling variables often produces trivial and banal findings.

g) Quantitative research is not totally objective because the researcher is already subjective in choosing a particular problem while neglecting others, and in the interpretation of the results by, for instance, trying to 'prove' that the findings agree with what other researchers found.

Ignoring the limitation of the mechanistic approach of the quantitative research coupled with that of regarding 'facts' obtained from quantitative studies as true and same for all people and times, could be responsible for the failures being met by organizations, governments and even businesses that seek to generalize research findings and apply them to people with different socio—cultural backgrounds, beliefs, economic status and aspirations. Sometimes, quantitative research reduces human beings to machines by attempting to predict human behavior using econometrics and other quantitative techniques to explain human behaviour which is fluid, complex and largely unpredictable. The last limitation of quantitative or empirical research stated above (i.e. researcher's subjectivity) has also been pointed out by Harris (1979) when explaining the limitations of empiricism by stating that an investigator's pre-conception and motives influence his/her choice of methodology of investigation, and this affects the outcome of the study.

8.3 Qualitative Research Designs

Qualitative research deals with the investigation of a phenomenon in its natural setting in order to understand and interpret it adequately and through the perspective of the research subjects. In the 1900s, some researchers rejected positivism and embraced the qualitative research paradigm. In the 1970s and 1980s, several academic journals with qualitative focus emerged, while in the 1990s the concept of a passive observer/researcher assumed in empirical studies was rejected, qualitative research became more participatory and researchers began to use mix methods (http://en.wikipedia.org/wiki/Qualitative_Research).

The qualitative research paradigm is based on the philosophy that reality is subjective because individuals and societies create their own reality, and on post—positivism. Post—positivism, also called post—empiricism, is an amendment to positivism, not a rejection of the scientific method. Post—positivism is the belief that theories, background, values and knowledge of the researcher can influence what is observed; and that reality can be known only with imperfection and probabilities (http://en.m.wikipedia.org/wiki/Postpositivism).

Qualitative data takes the form of video recordings, sound recordings, photographs, transcripts of interviews, minutes of meeting, dairies, teachers' lesson notes, field notes from observations, records of litigations and court rulings, TV shows, contents of websites, blogs, etc.

Some of the limitations of qualitative research are that it is "harder, more stressful and time consuming" and only suitable for people who care about it and take it seriously. In addition, establishing conventional standards of reliability and validity is very difficult, and researcher's presence has effect on the subjects (Hughes, 2006).

The methods of qualitative research include the following:

a) *Phenomenology:* this is a study of a phenomenon aimed at describing subjective reality as perceived by the sample of the population being studied.

b) *Grounded theory method:* this is an inductive research method developed by Barney Glasser and Anselm Straus in 1967. Its fundamental property is that anything that reaches the hands of a researcher in the course of studying a phenomenon is data. The steps followed in grounded theory are i) data collection, ii) data coding, iii) grouping of codes into similar concepts, iv) forming categories from concepts, v) using categories as basis for creating theory or generating hypotheses (http://en.m.wikipedia.org/wiki/Grounded_Theory).

c) *Methods of data analysis:* content analysis is used in analyzing qualitative data. It involves studying each part of the collected data with a view to rearranging it in some order, classifying, summarizing, coding and tabulating it, and where applicable, calculating averages, percentages, and standard deviations as well as drawing charts. This allows the researcher to describe the data. Next, the researcher makes inferences or derives some meanings, implications or conclusion from the data

d) *Methods of ensuring the credibility/validity of findings*: Internal validity of qualitative studies is measured by looking at the accuracy of description of data, referring results to peers for vetting and review, and referring results back to respondents for confirmation of findings before publishing them (Sambo, 2005). Corroboration is also used to ensure that research findings accurately reflect peoples' perception, whatever they may be. Triangulation in form of convergence of multiple data from multiple data collection sources and use of multiple researchers investigating the same phenomenon is another method of ensuring validity of findings. Other methods are research audit, peer debriefing, etc, (Key, 1997). Peer debriefing is among the validation methods created by Yvonna S. Lincoln and Egon S. Guba. It requires a researcher to have meetings with professional colleagues with impartial views about the study. During these meeting the research method used, the data collected, exhibits obtained, photographs taken and the research report are all examined (http://www.debriefing.com/peer.debriefing/).

There are many qualitative research designs which include the following:

1. *Historical Research/Archival Methods:* This is undertaken to arrive at an accurate account of past events to see how they are related to present events and to predict the future trends of events. Historical sources include documents, archives and archaeological remains such as tools, utensils and weapons.

2. *Survey Research:* A survey research studies the present and is meant to determine the status of a given phenomenon rather than to identify causative factors. Survey research involves both large and small population samples. One advantage of survey research is that it investigates phenomena in their natural setting.

3. *Case studies:* Case studies involve detailed investigations of individuals, groups, institutions and other social units. They differ from survey in terms of a closer and detailed study of only one or few individuals, institutions or systems.

4. *Unobtrusive Research:* This takes the form of content analysis, for instance the contents of newspapers and magazines within a given period or after a national event such as presidential election. Contents of blogs created by youth can be studied to determine popular or rare themes receiving attention or the kinds of aspirations or frustrations expressed by youth.

5. *Focus Group Discussion:* This involves a researcher facilitating and moderating discussion on a given topic or issue with a small group that is neither too large to prevent

some members from participating nor too small to limit the amount of information to be collected. A group of 5-10 people could be alright.

6. *Action research:* In an action research the researcher systematically finds solution to a problem by working together with the research subjects, collecting data on cyclical bases and refining methodological tools to suit the situation. The main goals of this approach to research are to solve real problems, turn people into researchers, make them learn something in the best way and enable them to apply what they have learned. Kurt Lewin coined the term action research in 1946, today it is also called participatory research, emancipatory research, action learning, etc, (O'Brien, 2001). Problems of truancy by primary school pupils, corruption and injustice among community leaders, outbreak of diseases due to poor sanitation, low demand for perishable farm produce, etc, can be solved together with the affected people using action research.

7. *Ethnography:* This research design is used to explore and graphically explain the culture of a people from their own point of view. Data collection methods used by ethnographers include interviews, participant observations, field notes, use of local informants and sometimes living among the people whose culture is being studied.

8. *Interviewing:* This is the use of detailed, semi-structured and sometimes unstructured interviews to gain deep understanding of a phenomenon. It is not the same as the structured or short interviews used to collect quantitative data.

9. *Biography:* This is a study that focuses on life patterns, achievements and experiences of individuals operating within social and historical contexts. Biographical data are collected during the course of lengthy semi-structured interviews and through the analysis of documents. Biographical studies can be undertaken by students of history, economics and religious studies to find out the achievements and

experiences of great people in the areas of leadership, business and preaching respectively. Students of language can also be asked to undertake biographical studies to develop their literary skills.

10. *Observation*: There are two types of observations. In participant observation, a researcher becomes a member of a group, culture or setting being studied and conforms to its rules. In non-participant observation, data is collected by observing the behaviour of research subjects without interaction with them. A researcher can investigate bargaining process taking place in a cattle market through participant observation by selling or buying a cow and by acting as cattle dealer. Alternatively, the researcher can simply sit in a corner to observe the bargaining process or use a video camera to record the process.

11. *Philosophical research:* This type of research uses intellectual analysis to clarify definitions, concepts, identify ethics or make value judgments on issues related to a field of study.

12. *Visual Methods:* This is the use of video to record social life. Here researchers are not just concerned with the activities and interactions of human bodies but also with how subjects interact with physical artefacts. They may use the recorded images and sound either as a resource for analysis or for the documentation and representation of those actions to other audiences (Adamu, 2012).

13. *Textual analysis:* this investigates the ways in which members of various cultures and subcultures make sense of who they are and of how they fit into the world in which they live. It is useful for researchers working in cultural studies, media studies, in mass communication, and perhaps even in sociology and philosophy. A text is something that we make meaning from, it includes books, cartoons, films, television

programs, magazines, advertisements, clothes, graffiti, etc. All these can be studied in order to obtain a sense of the ways in which particular people at particular times, make sense of the world around them (Adamu, 2012).

It should be noted that a particular research can be carried out by combining two or more research designs; it all depends on the research topic and goals.

8.4 Sampling Methods

Population and its Sample

In research, the term population refers to the entire set of a given group under study; it could include group of people, events as well as living and non-living things. This means that there is a population of students in a college, rivers in a country, lions in a forest, etc. A population is finite if it has a known number, and infinite if the number is too large to be known precisely.

A sample is that portion of a population which is studied closely in order to gain some knowledge and make generalization about the population it represents. A sample is drawn from a population after a clear definition of the population by identifying the characteristics of its members. The use of samples in research minimizes cost and saves time.

Probability Sampling Techniques

Probability sampling techniques are used when the population is finite, the probability of selection of samples is known and an estimate of the sampling error (degree of departure) can be made. A study on the attitude of final year students of Usmanu Dafodio University to self-employment, for example, has a finite population because the exact number of the students could be known. Other conditions for the use of the probability sampling technique are that every member in the population must have an equal opportunity of being selected, and the selection of any member must have no influence on the selection of any other member. The probability sampling techniques include the following:

a. *Random Sampling:* With this, each person or item has an equal chance of being included in the sample. The sample can be drawn by assigning numbers to individuals. The numbers are written on pieces of paper and then mixed, the required sample is drawn. Alternatively, a table of computer generated random numbers could be used. Some calculators also have random numbers.

b. *Systematic Sampling:* This is used when the elements of population are arranged in a sequential order and a sample is drawn based on a predetermined way or system. In a school, for instance, students' names are listed serially or alphabetically. A sample can be drawn the population of students by using a system of including every 4th name on the on list until the required sample size is attained.

c. *Stratified Random Sampling:* This requires the separation of population elements into non-overlapping groups called strata. This is done to ensure that sub-groups are represented in the sample. The final year students of Makerere University in Uganda, for instance, can be divided into stratum on the basis of their age, sex, state of origin, departments, social status, etc, depending on researcher's interest. A simple random sampling is then used within each stratum.

d. *Cluster Sampling:* This is also called area sampling and is simply a random sample in which each sampling unit is a collection or a cluster. Local governments in a state, hamlets in a city and halls of residence in a university could be regarded as clusters.

Non -probability Sampling Techniques

With non-probability sampling techniques, a researcher cannot estimate sampling error and generalize research findings beyond the sample studied. However, if the study is repeated and the results are not significantly different, generalizations could be accepted.

The non-probability sampling techniques stated by Bailey (1994) are explained below with relevant examples:

1. *Convenience Sampling*: An investigator simply chooses the closest persons, as respondents in order to save time and money. A researcher working in an organization, can use its staff to get the sample required for a study without going to distant places thereby spending more money and consuming more time and energy.

2. *Quota Sampling:* Respondents are drawn from different quotas to be represented in the sample. Examples of such quotas are ethnic groups, geographical locations and social classes.

3. *Dimensional Sampling*: This is a multi-dimensional form of quota sampling. It is suitable for a small scale study. A researcher specifies all dimensions (variables) of interest in the population and then ensures that every combination of the dimensions is represented by at least one case. A researcher interested in comparing the incomes of farmers, artisans, teachers and landlords living in a given area, can use this sampling technique to represent each category of people in the sample.

4. *Purposive or Judgmental Sampling*: A researcher can use his research skill and prior knowledge to choose respondents that will best meet the purpose of the study. A researcher studying the attitudes of households to a new brand of cooking oil can pick his/her sample from known users of the product to suit the purpose of the study. Total population sampling, also called total coverage sampling, is a type of purposive sampling technique where a researcher examines the entire population of his/her study because the size of the population that has a particular characteristic of research interest is relatively small (Laerd Dissertation, nd). A researcher interested on the challenges that 23 newly appointed school principals face in school administration in a given region or community can use the total

population sampling technique because the school principals having the characteristic of *being newly appointed* are only 23.

5. *Snowball or chain referred sampling*: This is suitable for studying deviant sub-cultures where respondents may not be visible. A study involving drug addicts may require snowball sampling. The sample is drawn in stages. At the first stage few respondents with the required characteristics are interviewed and used as informants to identify other respondents with the same characteristics. This continues till when the required sample size is obtained.

The Occasional Sampling Technique

Sulaiman (2009) adds what he calls *occasional sampling technique* to the non-probability sampling techniques. This technique involves the use of participants attending an occasion as samples of a population they represent. It differs from the convenience sampling technique explained above. The main difference is that for the occasional sampling technique, the opportunity for involving the sample of respondents in a study exists for a short period of time. Some of the merits of the occasional sampling technique are that it saves time and money because research subjects are found in a single place; secondly, the respondents tend to be more co-operative during occasions as they seek recognition and attention than when they are met in their business premises. One of the demerits of the technique is that only experienced researchers can design and conduct studies at a short notice as some occasions are made known to the public few days to their occurrence. Secondly, occasions are not suitable for the use of interviews or questionnaires loaded with many questions as people in attendance usually have many things to attend to. Example of occasions that provide a researcher with opportunities to get samples include orientation camps, venues of national conferences and workshops, market sessions on village market days, trade fairs, exhibitions, etc.

Sulaiman used the occasional sampling technique to sample out eight (8) participants in the first edition of the Global Agricultural

Extension tagged 'Kano 2009', in conducting a study on the nature and economic implications of Appropriate Technology for Agriculture in Kano State, Nigeria. The result of this study had already been published as a journal article (refer to Sulaiman, 2011).

Determining Appropriate Sample Size

To permit generalization about the population it represents, a sample must have an appropriate size. In using a sample, a researcher must accept some level of risk of being wrong when making inference about the population on the basis of information derived from the sample. The level of risk relates directly to the size of the sample, therefore the less risk a researcher is willing to take, the larger his/her sample must be. The size of a population, types of variables involved in a study (continuous or categorical), research design and type of statistical analysis to be used, all determine the appropriate sample size for a study. Qualitative research designs, for instance, can have very few samples because they use non-probability sampling technique. Case studies and biographies, for example, can involve a single organization or individual. Quantitative research designs require the use of sample sizes that are large enough to permit generalizations.

Bartlet, Kotrlik, and Higgins, (2001) used the formula devised in 1977 by W. G.Cochran for determining sample size for both continuous and categorical data, to construct a sample size table for continuous and categorical data. The table, for instance, gives the following sample sizes for populations with the sizes given in table 6.1 (the entire table is available at http://www.osra.org/itlpj/bartlettkotrlikhiggins.pdf.). Krejcie and Morgan (1970) had also used a formula construct a similar table for determining required sample size for research activities.

Table 8.1 Extracts of Sample sizes for continuous and categorical data

Population size	Sample size for continuous data with 0.03 margin of error, α = 0.05, t =1.96	Sample size for categorical data with 0.05 margin of error, p = 0.50, t =1.96
100	55	80
400	92	196
1,000	106	278
4,000	119	351
10,000	119	351

(Source: Bartlett, Kotrlik, & Higgins, 2001)

The type of statistics to be used for data analysis also needs to be considered in determining appropriate sample sizes. The Kruskal-Wallis test, for instance, needs a sample with a least 5 members or observations. As for multiple regression analysis, most authors recommend that you should have at least 10 to 20 times as many observations (cases, respondents) as you have variables; otherwise the estimates of the regression line are probably very unstable and unlikely to replicate if you were to conduct the study again (http://www.statsoft.com/textbook/multiple-regression).

8.5 Data Collection Methods

Primary and Secondary Data

A researcher collects data with a view to testing hypothesis or answering research questions. The data could be primary or secondary. It is primary when it is used for the purpose for which it is collected. Data used for a purpose other than that for which it is collected is called a secondary data. Data collected and compiled by Central Bank of India or the Bureaus of Statistics in Nigeria is secondary data to a researcher but a primary data to the institutions that have collected it.

Continuous and Discreet Data

Continuous data or variable is one that increases steadily in fractions or has an unlimited number of intermediate values. Examples of continuous data or variables are age, height, velocity and time. They take more than one value along a continuum.

Discreet data or variable takes on a finite number of values. Sex, military rank and number of children in a family are discreet variables. Discreet data has a single constant value and its value is expressed in quantitative terms (e.g. 14 children) or by word of label (e.g. a male receptionist, a graduate, a red car, etc).

Types of Data Measurement Scales

Measurement refers to giving a number to objects, attributes, conditions, etc, using a set of rules to ensure consistency and reliability. Measurement is akin to an operational definition which a researcher uses to define terms in the context of his/her research work. If, for instance, one is conducting a study on the effect of a new irrigation method on crop yield or of a new teaching method on students' abilities, one has to adopt appropriate measures for crop yield (e.g. kilograms, bags, grams, etc) and for students' abilities (e.g. raw examination marks, Grade Point Averages, etc).

Measurement scales are ways in which data or variables are defined and categorized. Each type of scale has its own appropriate statistical tool of analysis. Classical measurement theory recognises four levels of measurement: categorical (nominal), ordinal, interval, and ratio. They are explained as follows:

1. *Nominal Scale:* If sets or populations of things are classified into categories in such a way that no two categories are the same, and numbers are used to stand for each category, a nominal scale is used. For example, in a family, there are two categories of members, male and female. A researcher can use 1 for male and 2 for female, or if there are red, white, blue and yellow balls in a school, the numbers 1,2,3,4 can be used to represent them respectively. When a data set has only two categories they are called *dichotomous* variables, but when the categories are more than two they are called *polytomous* variables. Variables such as gender, educational qualification, ethnicity, religion, race, colour are measured in a nominal scale.

2. *Ordinal Scale:* This scale uses an ordered series of relationship between a set of things. The elements of the set or members of a population are classified into categories and the categories are ordered, for instance, the red ball is bigger than the white ball, the yellow ball is the biggest of all, etc. A researcher can assign the number 1 to the biggest ball through to 4 for the smallest one, or vice versa. The Likert scale is an example of an ordinal scale.

3. *Interval Scale:* This is a measurement scale used for continuous data or variables such as age, height, and time. A researcher can measure the weights of samples of livestock taken from different farms using different values on the measurement scale to represent the weight of each unit in the sample. Such values can be assigned numbers like 0.25 kg, 0.75kg, 1.0kg, 1.7kg, 2.9kg, etc, when weighing fish or cockerels. The weights can be compared and analyzed through the arithmetical manipulations of addition, subtraction, division and multiplication. This cannot directly

9 Requirements for Quality Research & Academic Papers

be possible with a nominal or ordinal scale. Interval scale can have 0 as a point of measurement, temperature, for instance, can be 4^0 Celsius, 0^0 Celsius and -12^0 Celsius.

4. *Ratio Scale:* This scale is also used for continuous data such as age, height and time. It permits comparison of differences of values, but unlike the interval scale, this scale has an absolute or a fixed zero value (i.e. values not below 0). The researcher weighing cockerels cannot have a cockerel with a weight of 0.0kg among the samples taken because such type of cockerel does not exist at all. Similarly, it is not possible to have a student with zero intelligent quotients (IQ) or a tree with 0.0cm height as a sample from a population of students and trees, respectively.

The Major Data Collection Methods

Data collection methods include the following:

1. Questionnaire

A questionnaire is a data collection instrument and method comprising questions designed for respondents to answer. There are two types of questionnaires, the structured and the open-ended questionnaire. In the structured questionnaire a respondent answers a question by simply choosing what he regards as the appropriate answer from options provided. The open-ended questionnaire provides spaces for respondents to write their answers. With structured questionnaire, data is quantified easily, but when it comes to obtaining information, which a researcher may not even expect from respondents, the open-ended questions are better. A researcher can use a combination of both types of questions in a single questionnaire to obtain better results.

A researcher can also use *intensity questions* to measure the strength of a respondent's feeling, attitude or opinion in relation to a particular person, topic, issue, policy, etc. Such questions allow the researcher to obtain more quantitative information about respondents, for instance, instead of a finding that 70 percent of respondents are in favour a given policy, one can obtain results showing 20 percent of them are strongly in favour while 50 percent are mildly in favour. The Likert-type answer scale is the most common and easily used intensity question that allows respondents to choose one of several degrees of feeling about a statement from strong approval to strong disapproval (Air University Sampling and Surveying Handbook, 2002).

Questions contained in questionnaires should be relevant to the problem for which they are designed. They need to be short and clear; respondents may not have sufficient time to respond to a questionnaire that is too demanding. Double – barrel and leading questions should be avoided, the former are questions with more than one answer while the latter suggest answers expected from the respondents.

2. Interviews

With an interview, a researcher or an enumerator assisting him/her is having a face-to-face encounter with a respondent. Questions that are not understood by the respondent could be reframed or made clearer. In comprehending responses, the researcher may utilize the respondent's gestures or body language which questionnaires will never show.

Interviews become necessary when subjects are illiterate or too old to read and write. One problem with interviews is that the researcher's mannerism, dressing and method of approach could affect the responses. Interviews are time consuming especially when a large sample of respondents is involved. Interviews should be standardized and structured to ensure uniformity. Interview schedules should be prepared before conducting interviews. Tape recorders, tablet computers, handsets and other devices can be used to record interviews to avoid loss of information and asking respondents to answer questions repeatedly.

3. Observation

A researcher can collect primary data by personally observing what his / her subjects are doing or how a given system operates. Traffic volume in a section of a town, social interaction between junior and senior students in a boarding school, and late coming by workers in a factory could all be directly observed by a researcher. Observation as a data collection tool has some limitations, for instance the presence of the observer may change the behavior of the subjects. Secondly, observation is time-consuming.

4. Tests

Tests are also means of collecting primary data. Tests are conducted to collect data on patients attending hospitals and clinics. Such data may include types and frequency of diseases diagnosed through blood, urine and widal tests, etc. In the field of education, tests for intelligence and aptitudes are also means of gathering data. In the natural sciences there is, for instance, the soil test, while in the social and management sciences, there are, for example, liquidity test for a business and performance test for the personnel of an organization.

Pre-testing and Reviewing Questions

Questions formulated by a researcher may have certain problems which he/she may not be aware of. When questionnaires are administered to few respondents to identify flaws before administering them to the sampled respondents, they are being pre —tested. Interview questions are also pre-tested for the same purpose.

With the pre—testing of questions, the kind of mistakes that may be detected include following:

a) Some questions may be redundant.
b) Spaces provided for some open-ended questions may be insufficient.
c) Some questions may be ambiguous.
d) Some important questions that need to be asked may be left out.
e) A significant number of respondents may be unable to respond to some questions and simply write "don't know" and this could affect the sample size.

Questions are then reviewed or modified based on the results of pre-tests.

Word of Advice

It is advisable for researchers to submit their questionnaires and interview questions to qualified and experienced people for assessment and validation.

8.6 Methods of Data Analysis

Summary and Presentation of Data

Both primary and secondary data collected by a researcher need to be summarized and presented in a suitable form to permit analysis and inference. The responses contained by hundreds of questionnaires, for example, have to be summarized and sometimes coded or reduced. Data reduction is the process of reducing data to some form for suitable analysis. Coding can take the form of assigning numbers to expected responses (pre-coding) or to obtained responses (post-coding) and is necessary especially when a computer is to be used to analyze the data.

The summarized or coded data is presented in various forms usually in Chapter Four of students' project reports. Tables and charts are common ways of presenting data, they need to be labeled and numbered for easy reference (e.g. Table 4.1 Respondents' Hobbies). Sometimes, depending on the research design and the nature of questions put to research subjects, the responses are summarized and presented in words rather than in figures or in form of charts.

Forms and Uses of Data Analysis

Data analysis takes many forms which depend on the use for which the analysis is made. If the analysis is required for descriptive purposes or for answering research questions, descriptive statistics could be used to analyze the data.

Measures of central tendency (mean. median and mode), measures of dispersion (range, quartile deviation, standard deviation and variance) and percentages fall under descriptive statistics. Descriptive statistics are suitable for descriptive or exploratory researches as they are meant to describe situations and events rather than to determine cause - effect relationships. Uses of descriptive statistics, as stated by Selltiz, Wrightsman and Cook (1976), include the following:

1. *Characterizing what is "typical" of a sample:* Statistical data gathered from a sample of textile firms in Ghana in relation to their staff strength, capital base, range of products, profits and sales volume can, for instance, provide typical features of textile firms in the country. Mean profit, median capital base and other descriptive statistics can be used to describe the sample.

2. *Indicating how widely individuals in the group or sample vary:* Using the above example, measures of dispersion can be used to find out the extent to which the profit obtained by a textile firm varies with or deviates from the mean profit. These measures include:

    a) Quartile deviation showing points within which the central half of observed cases fall if data correspondents to an ordinal scale.
    b) Standard deviation measuring the average distance of individuals from the group mean.

c) Range indicating the range of variation in the group.

d) Variance measuring dispersion. It is obtained by squaring a standard deviation.

3. *Showing the relationship between different variables in a data:* For instance, the relationship between sales volume and profitability can, for instance, be shown with the use of ratios.

4. *Describing differences among two or more groups of individuals*: For instance, differences between firms located in an urban area and those located in villages could also be described by using descriptive statistics such as percentages and ratios.

It should be noted that descriptive statistics are not used for testing hypotheses, unless if they are combined with statistics of inference.

Statistics of inference are used to deduce the truth or falsity of a hypothesis. The inference to be tested could be that some phenomenon that is true for a sample is also true for the population from which it was drawn. The aim is to gain some information about a population by relying on its sample.

Statistics of inference are divided into parametric and non-parametric statistics. A parameter is a feature of a population that includes population mean, standard deviation and proportion. Parametric statistics assume that data come from a given type of probability distribution from which inferences are made. Other assumptions are that scores in a population are normally distributed about the mean, and that scores being used come from interval or continuous data. Examples of parametric statistics are Z- test, t-test, F-test, ANOVA, Pearson correlation, regression, etc. A researcher should use non-parametric statistics if the above assumptions are violated.

Non-Parametric statistics are distribution-free. They include Spearman rank correlation coefficient, chi-square test, Binomial test, run test, contingency tables, Kruskal-Wallis test, etc. Non-Parametric statistics are also used to test hypotheses and to make inferences.

The interpretation of statistical results and the drawing of conclusions are also part of data analysis. It is very essential for researchers, users and evaluator of research reports to consider the following questions which determine the quality of data analysis.

(a) Have the assumptions or conditions required for adopting a particular research design been met?
(b) Are the statistical procedures relevant and are the results appropriately interpreted?
(c) Does the researcher distinguish between statistical significance and practical significance?

A statistical significance does mean that the relationship between given variables is necessarily important or significant in a real sense, it only indicates that we can be sure within a statistical margin of error that such a relationship exists (Bailey, 1994).

Precautions against Types of Errors in Research

Bailey (1994) identifies some common errors in research which are committed at different stages of the research process. They need to be avoided. They are as follows:

1. *Concept and hypotheses construction stage*: The errors could be improper definition of concepts being measured, meaning that there is no face validity. If, for example, a researcher investigating effect of inflation on welfare of people in some selected countries ends up covering and reporting causes or types of inflation, has committed this error. The errors could also be in the formulation of hypothesis.

2. *The stage of constructing research instrument:* The error could be in terms of lack of reliability of data due to faulty or ambiguous wording of questions used in a questionnaire or any other instrument used to collect data.

3. *Sampling stage:* The common error is lack of external validity, that is, non- representation of population from which a sample is drawn.

4. *Data gathering stage***:** Error could be due to environmental factors, effect of research instrument, personal characteristics of respondents and their relationship with the researcher.

5. *Coding stage***:** In coding data, incorrect information may be recorded due to missing data, coding error and illegible hand writing.

6. *Data analysis stage:* The error could be due to misuse of statistics, faulty interpretations of results and wrong conclusions.

Hypothesis Testing Errors

Type I error is committed when a researcher rejects a null hypothesis when it should be retained. The probability of committing this error is small and is denoted by alpha (α). With a 5% significance level there is only a 5% risk of rejecting what should be accepted.

Reducing the significance level to 1% will minimize the error but the lower the significance level the higher the risk of committing another error (type II error). Type II error occurs when a null hypothesis is accepted instead of being rejected. This error is bigger than type I error and is denoted by beta (β).

Type III error is the most insidious of statistical decision errors. It involves correctly concluding that the null hypothesis should be rejected but attributing the source of the effect to the wrong treatment.

The use of large samples and repeating a study several times are ways of reducing hypothesis testing errors.

The Need to Ensure Validity in Research

Validity in research simply refers to the degree to which a research instrument or statistical technique measures what it is suppose to measure. There are various measures used in research depending on what is being measured. A measure of correlation should not be used to measure attitude, just as a ruler should not be used to measure the weight of a child. Edward Carmines and Richard Zeller cited in Babbie (1986) identified the three types of validity in research, which are explained below:

- Criteria-related or predictive validity: this refers to the extent to which a test or any research instrument can forecast future performance of research subjects. A driving test for instance, has predictive validity if the results could be used to predict driving ability of the tested individuals.
- Content validity: this is the extent to which a measure covers the range of concepts, skills or abilities relevant to a given task. A driving test that excludes some essentials skills like reversing a vehicle has no content validity.
- Construct validity: a construct is anything created by the mind, it can be an idea, a concept or an attribute of something; it is different from a physical object that embodies the idea, the concept or the attribute respectively. Construct validity is the extent to which a measure relates to the construct being measured on the basis existing theories. It is theoretically known that the intelligent quotient (IQ), for instance, is used to measure child's intelligence, if a researcher uses it to measure child's attitude to learning a foreign language, the research lacks construct validity.

Chapter Nine

DEFINING TERMS AND COMPILING REFERENCES

Chapter Objectives

By the time you finish reading this chapter, which covers the 9th requirement for producing quality research and academic papers, it is expected that you will be able to

- Operationally define key terms related to a research topic or problem.
- Explain the difference between reference and bibliography.
- Compile references based on stipulated citation and reference styles.

9.1 Definition of Terms

One is expected to give operational definitions of some important terms that appear in a research topic, problem statement, objectives, findings or any part of the research report. An operational definition of these terms refers to their special meaning in the context of the research report, not their ordinary or dictionary meanings.

The topic, *The Contribution of Markets to the Revenue of Bichi Local Government: A Case Study of Bichi, Badume and Saye Markets,* which was coined by Sulaiman (2012a), has also been used by him to illustrate the definition of terms. In this regard, the terms that require operational definition include *contribution, market, revenue, federation account* and *efficacy of revenue collection.* Their operational definitions were given as follows:

> *Contribution:* addition made by the revenue collected from the three markets to the total revenue of Bichi Local Government from 2006 — 2011.

Market: places where buyers and sellers of goods and services meet on designated days of the week (Sundays and Wednesday for Badume market and Fridays for Bichi and Saye markets) to transact business.

Revenue from Federation Account: this refers to what Bichi Local Government collected as grant from the Federal Government of Nigeria from 2006 — 2011.

Efficacy of revenue of collection: the effectiveness and efficiency with which revenue is collected from the markets included in the study.

You can see that you cannot get any of these definitions from any dictionary. It is the researcher that will decide on what each term means in the research proposal, and later, the report so that readers will understand it very well.

9.2 Reference Styles

One is expected to provide a list of all works that have been consulted in the course of conducting a research or literature review. This list, which is arranged alphabetically, is called a reference. Referencing serves a least three purposes: it can be used to support facts and arguments put forward by an author, to recognize and acknowledge sources of facts and ideas cited in a text, and lastly, to enable readers of the text to read more about what is cited. All works that have been cited in the report must appear in the references.

A bibliography is different from a reference because, in addition to the list of books referred to by a researcher; it contains titles of related books for further reading by readers of the report, which the researcher has not cited in it.

There are many reference styles in use depending on the choice of an institution, a publisher or a professional body. Whatever style is used, the reference needs to show author's name, year of publication, title of the work and edition (if any), name of the publisher and place of publication. Examples of reference styles used by publishers and associations are:

(1) Chicago University Press style.
(2) Modern Languages Association style.
(3) American Psychological Association (APA) style
(4) American Journal of Islamic Social Sciences (AJISS) style.
(5) Samarib Publishers style

You need to visit the web sites of these organizations to get the latest versions of their reference styles. If you are student writing a thesis, you need to get the approved citation and reference style of the institution to which you are submitting the thesis.

An Illustration of References based on the Samarib Publishers Style (SPS)

The following hypothetical examples illustrate how references are written using the SPS style (Sulaiman: 2012b):

Textbook

Adebayo, Kenneth O. (1990) 4th ed. *Methods of Social Science Research,* (Ibadan: The Blue Bird Press).

A Journal Article:

Ridwan, Balarabe (2001). "The Impact of the Perennial Fuel Scarcity on Economic Productivity in Katsina State," *Samarib Journal of Social and Management Sciences,* Vol. 2, No.1, 2001.

A Chapter from a Reader:

Akpan, Etim A. and Makarfi, Salisu B. (1999). "Cement Production in Nigeria: Problems and Prospects" in Okeke Nwachukwu (ed) *Perspectives in Building Technology* (Kano: Samarib Publishers).

For magazines and newspaper articles, the name of the author (if available) title of the article, date and name of the magazine or newspaper is required. For research reports the institutions to which the reports are submitted must be stated in addition to author's name, year and title, e.g.:

Ahmed, Garba S. (2011). *Cognitive Intelligence and Job Performance among Female Secondary School Teachers in Kogi State.* Unpublished thesis submitted to the Post-Graduate School, Bayero University, Kano, for the Award of Doctor of Philosophy in Educational Psychology.

For Internet/online publications, the complete web link to the published material with the date of access must be provided, e.g.:

Sulaiman, Sa'idu (2009) *Globoeconomic Policies for Overcoming the Current Global Recession,* retrieved on June 3, 2009 from http://www.scribd.com/doc/16068730/Globoeconomic-Policies-for-Overcoming-the-Current-Global-Recession

REFERENCES

Adamu, Abdullah U (2002) *Research Methodology in Humanities*, a paper presented at the two-day workshop entitled Academic Research Design/Development and Writing organized by COEASU in collaboration with NCCE and TETFUND from 26th -27th September 2012 and conducted at Hydro Hotel, Minna, Niger State.

Air University Sampling and Surveying Handbook. Revised (PDF) Edition: May 2002 retrieved on December 27, 2012 from http://www.au.af.mil/au/awc/awcgate/edref/smpl-srv.pdf

Babbie, Earl (1986), 4th ed. *The Practice of Social Research,* (California: Wadsworth Publishing Company.

Bailey, Kenneth D. (1994) 4th ed. *Method of Social Research,* (New York: The Free Press).

Bartlet, James E.; Kotrlik, Joe W. and Higgins, Chadwick C (2001). "Organizational Research: Determining Appropriate Sample Size in Survey Research". *Information Technology, Learning, and Performance Journal,* Vol. 19, No. 1, Spring 2001 retrieved on December 23rd from http://www.osra.org/itlpj/bartlettkotrlikhiggins.pdf

Gocsik, Karen (2004) What Is an Academic Paper? Dartmouth College. Retrieved on June 21, 2008 from www.dartmouth.edu/~writing/materials/student/ac_paper/what.shtml

Grounded Theory, retrieved on July 24, 2012 from http://en.m.wikipedia.org/wiki/Grounded_Theory

Guidelines on Writing a Philosophy Paper, retrieved on July 21, 2012 from http://www.jimpryor.net/teaching/guidelines/writing.html

Harris, Kevin (1979). *Education and Knowledge,* (London: Routledge and Kegan Paul).

http://dictionary.reference.com/browse/plagiarism Accessed on June 15, 2012.

http://www.informs.org/Find-Research-Publications/Journals/Author-Portal/Publications-Policies/Guidelines-for-Copyright-Plagiarism
Accessed on June 14, 2012.

Hughes, Christina L. (2006). *Quantitative and Qualitative Approaches,* Retrieved on December 13, 2012 from *http://www.warwick.ac.uk/fac/soc/sociology/..../quantitativequalitative/*

Key, James P. (1997). *Research Design in Occupational Education,* retrieved on December 27, 2012 from http://www.okstate.edu/ag/agedcm4h/academic/aged5980a/5980/nwepage21.htm

Krejcie, Robert V and Morgan, Daryle W. (1970). "Determining Sample Size for Research Activities," *Educational and Psychological Measurement,* 1970, 30, 607-610. Retrieved on December 27, 2012 from
people.usd.edu/~mbaron/edad810/Krejcie.pdf

Laerd Dissertation, (nd) *Total Population Sampling* retrieved on September 2, 2016 from http:/dissertation.laerd.com/total-population-sample.php

Multiple Regression, retrieved on December 27, 2012 from
 http://www.statsoft.com/textbook/multiple-regression).

Numerical Analysis, retrieved on December 20, 2012 from
http://en.m.wikipedia.org/wiki/ Numerical _Analysis

O'Brien, Rory (2001). *An Overview of the Methodological Approach of Action Research,* retrieved on December 29' from
http://www.web.ca/robrien/papers/arfinal.html

Peer Debriefing, retrieved on December 20, 2012 from
 http://www.debriefing.com/peer.debriefing/.

Postpositivism, retrieved on December 20, 2012 from
http://en.wikipedia.org/wiki/Postpositivism

Qualitative Research, retrieved on December 20, 2012 from
http://en.wikipedia.org/wiki/Qualitative_Research

Rosenberg, Morris (1984). "Meaning of Relationship in Social Survey Analysis" Bulmer, Martin(ed) *Sociological Research Methods – An Introduction*, (London: The Macmillan Press).

Sambo, Abdussalami A. (2005). *Research Methods in Education*, (Ibadan: Stirling-Horden Publishers Nig. Ltd).

Sulaiman, Sa'idu (2009), *Occasional Sampling in Research*, Accessed on December 18, 2012 from http://www.scribd.com/doc/15492828/Occasional-Sampling-in-Research

Sulaiman, Sa'idu (2011), "Appropriate Technology for Agriculture in Kano State of Nigeria: Its Nature and Economic Implications" *The Kumbotso Teacher Educator: A Journal of Multidisciplinary Studies*, Vol.2 No.2 July 2011 (Kano: Sa'adatu Rimi College of Education, Kumbotso).

Sulaiman, Sa'idu (2012a) *The Research Process in the Social Sciences*, a paper presented on April 19, 2012 at a one-day seminar organised for the lecturers of the Department of Economics, Sa'adatu Rimi College of Education, Kumbotso, Kano, Nigeria.

Sulaiman, Sa'idu (2012b), *Researchers' Companion*, 2nd ed. (Kano: Samarib Publishers).

Sulaiman, Sa'idu (2013), *Originality, Plagiarism and Contribution to Knowledge in Academic Papers*, a paper presented at the Capacity Building Workshop on Writing Academic Papers organized by the Kumbotso Teacher Educator journal (KUTEJ) for the academic staff of the Sa'adatu Rimi College of Education Kumbotso, Kano, Nigeria and conducted from 23rd- 31st March 2016.

Selltiz, Clair; Wrigtsman, Lawrence S and Cook, Stuart W. (1976) 3rd ed. *Research Methods in Social Relations*, (HoltSounders-International Editions).

Syed, Ibrahim B. *Thinking Process* retrieved on April 6, 2015 from http://www.irfi.org/articles/articles_51_100/thinking_process.htm

Types of Articles Published, retrieved on July 20, 2012 from http://www.dsjie.org/dnn/AuthorCenter/TypesOfArticlesPublished.aspx

Types of Articles in Scholarly Journals, retrieved on July 20, 2012 from http://lfcc.libguides.com/content.php?pid=177721&sid=1502560

Types of journal manuscripts retrieved on July 21, 2012from http://www.springer.com/authors/journal+authors/journal+authors+acad emy?SGWID=0-1726414-12-837305-0

www.ingramcontent.com/pod-product-compliance
Lightning Source LLC
Chambersburg PA
CBHW060200290526
45789CB00003B/1096